FRIENDSHIP SALAD

written by Lynn Trepicchio
illustrated by Amy Ning

HARCOURT BRACE & COMPANY

Orlando Atlanta Austin Boston San Francisco Chicago Dallas New York
Toronto London

I have the bananas.

I have the apples.

I have the oranges.

I have the pineapples.

I have the bowl.
Let's put the fruit in it.

I have the spoon.
Let's mix it all together.

Our friendship salad is done.
Let's eat!